If I Had A Friend

BY: Cheryl A. Shyne

Cheryl Shyne
Enjoy

Copyright

ILLUSTRATOR: Muzamil Saleem

ISBN : Published and printed in the United States of America.

If I had a friend, we could ride our bikes together.

If I Had a Friend
by Cheryl A.Shyne

If I had a friend, we could play basketball together in the park.

If I had a friend, we could go to the beach and play in the sand together.

If I Had a Friend
by Cheryl A.Shyne

3

If I had a friend, we could play together with my new puppy.

If I Had a Friend
by Cheryl A.Shyne

4

If I had a friend, we could camp in a tent in my backyard and share scary stories.

If I Had a Friend
by Cheryl A.Shyne

If I had a friend, we could eat our favorite
Rice Krispie treats together.

If I Had a Friend
by Cheryl A.Shyne

6

If I had a friend, we could make a snowman together.

If I Had a Friend
by Cheryl A. Shyne

7

If I had a friend, we could play soccer together on the same team.

If I had a friend, we could celebrate our birthdays together.

If I Had a Friend
by Cheryl A. Shyne

9

If I had a friend, we could eat our favorite cookie dough ice cream together.

If I had a friend, we could play football together in my backyard.

If I Had a Friend
by Cheryl A.Shyne

If I had a friend, we could go water sliding together.

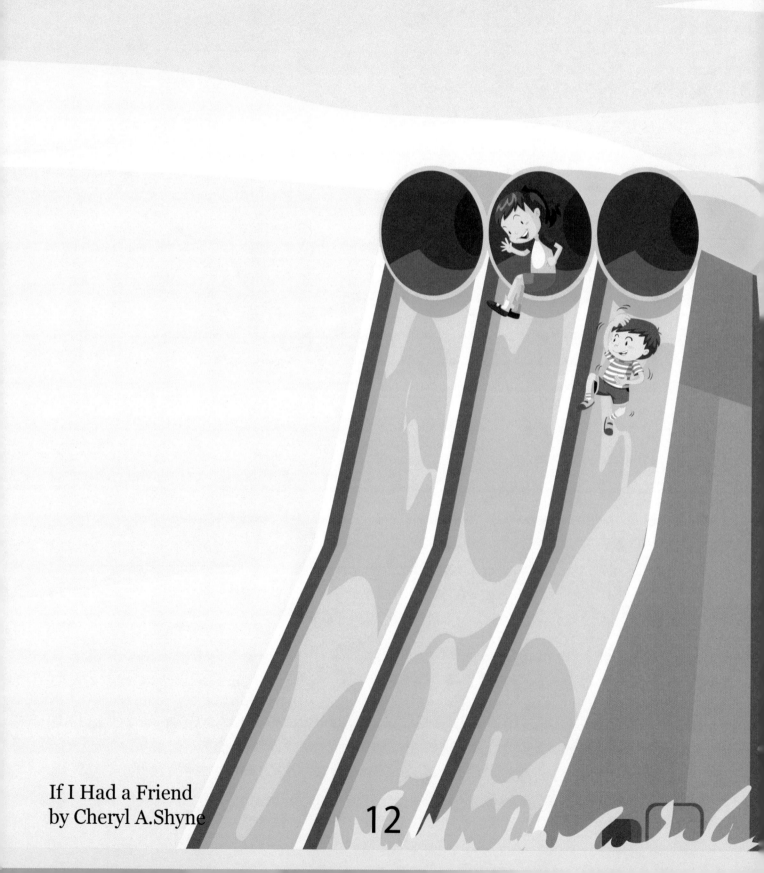

If I had a friend, we could watch spiderman together.

If I had a friend, we could create art projects together.

If I had a friend, we could sing a song on our bluetooth microphones together.

If I had a friend, we could bake chocolate chip cookies with our moms together.

If I Had a Friend
by Cheryl A.Shyne

If I had a friend, we could go roller skating together.

If I had a friend, we could go to Michigan Adventure Amusement Park together.

If I had a friend, we could go on a nature walk together with my big sister.

If I Had a Friend
by Cheryl A.Shyne

19

If I had a friend, we could eat our favorite chocolate sprinkled donut together.

If I had a friend, we could jump rope together.

If I Had a Friend
by Cheryl A.Shyne

If I had a friend, we could read our favorite book together "Spread Your Sunshine With Acts of Kindness."

If I had a friend, we could play Fortnite video game together.

If I had a friend, we could race up and down the street until we are out of breath. We would laugh and laugh.

If I had a friend, I could help him tie his shoes.

If I had a friend, we could play in leaves together.

If I had a friend,we could go to the neighborhood store and buy our favorite candy together.

If I had a friend, we could take our dogs for a walk together.

If I had a friend, it would bring me so much happiness. I would have someone to have fun with.

If I Had a Friend
by Cheryl A.Shyne

About the Author

Cheryl A . Shyne is a wife,mother and a grandmother. She is an elementary school teacher in Michigan. She has a Bachelor of Arts in Psychology, and a Master of Science with a Specialization in Clinical Psychology. She is a Professional Visual Artist,Life Coach, Seamtress and Author.

In her spare time she loves creating art and spending time with her family.Her favorite food is Spaghetti and Fried Rice. She loves watching black and white movies, and going for walks with her husband on a sun shiny day.

Made in the USA
Columbia, SC
01 May 2022

59760035R00020